RICE RICE BABY

#2

THE SECOND COMING OF RICED

50 RICE COOKER RECIPES

Dexter Poin

"OWNING A RICE COOKER HAS BEEN A LIFE CHANGING EXPERIENCE!"

UNCLE BEN

"I FOUND ZEN IN A RICE COOKER!"

AUNT JEMIMA

"I AM GOING TO MURDER DEXTER!"

RACHAEL RAY

HI - I - AM - DEXTER'S - NEW - ROBOT - AND - I -
HAVE - BEEN - ORDERED - TO - REPLACE - HIS -
NONSENSICAL - CHILDISH - INTRODUCTIONS –
WITH - A - MORE - ADULT – LIKE - NON –
COMEDIC - STRAIGHT – LACED -
INTRODUCTION - THAT -IS -GUARANTEED -TO -
NOT -ANGER - THE - MASSES. - WE - SINCERELY
- HOPE - YOU - ENJOY - AT - LEAST - 5 - RECIPES
- PROVIDED - OUT - OF - THE - 50. - WE -
WELCOME - YOU - INTO - THE - RECIPE -
JUNKIES - FAMILY - AND - HOPE - YOU - ENJOY -
COOKING - AS - MUCH - AS - WE - DO.
GOOD - DAY.

Table of Contents

Asparagus and Tofu

Mac and Cheese The Rice Cooker Way

Pomegranate Quinoa Salad

Jalapeno Bread

No Meat Black Bean Chili

Pomegranate Pear Halves

Shrimp with Lemon Risotto

Balsamic Dijon Chicken and Farro with Mushrooms

Wheat Berry Salad

Frittata and Summer Vegetables

Vegetable Hot Cakes

Crazy Cheesy Polenta

Easy Chicken Curry

Kimichi

Seafood Steamer Rice

Zesty Corn Dip

Whole Chicken

Clam Chowder

Traditional Hummus

Sweet Corn on the Cob

Steamed Sweet Potatoes

Southern Corn Pudding

Steamed Mussels with Black Bean Sauce

Steamed Green Beans

Butternut Squash Steamed

Spicy Cheese Dip

Lemongrass with Shrimp Soup

Spanish Rice

Spaghetti Squash and Kale with Pancetta

Smoked Salmon Frittata

Shrimp and Girts

Savory Lentils

Rice San Antonio Style

Potato and Salmon Gratin

Orange Marmalade

Pinto Beans

Rice Pineapple Pudding

Peppermint Truffles

Barley Pearled Stuffing

Pasta Carbonara

Orange Rice Pilaf

Midnight Omelet

Lemon Dill Rice

Classic Quiche

Brussels Sprouts with Walnut Oil

Vegetarian Easy Penne Peasy

Vegetarian Noodle Soup

Rice Thai Style

Swiss Rice Pie

Spanish Rice

Asparagus and Tofu

Calories: 174

Carbohydrates: 22 g

Protein: 13 g

Fat: 4.5 g

Ingredients:

½ Small Bunch of Asparagus – 1 ½-Inch Length

½ - 6 Ounce Block of Tofu – Chopped

½ Small Carrot – Peeled, Sliced

1 Clove of Garlic – Minced

2 Tbsp. of Oyster Sauce (Optional)

1 Tbsp. of Soy Sauce

1 tsp. of Vegetable Oil

1 tsp. of Sesame Seed Oil

1 tsp. of Mirin

1 tsp. of Honey

Directions:

In a large mixing bowl, add all of the ingredients and toss them together.

Put them on a heatproof plate.

Steam it for 15-20 minutes.

Mac and Cheese The Rice Cooker Way

Calories: 260

Carbohydrates: 36 g

Protein: 12 g

Fat: 7 g

Ingredients:

2 Cups of Pasta – Uncooked

1 ½ Cups of Chicken Stock – Low Sodium

1 tsp. of Salt

1 Cup of Milk

1 ½ Cups of Shredded Cheese

Directions:

Put the pasta, stock, and salt in the cooker for only 15 minutes.

Add in the cheese and the milk. Stir it well. Cook it for another 20 minutes.

You can add in broccoli to make it even tastier.

Pomegranate Quinoa Salad

Calories: 163

Carbohydrates: 23 g

Protein: 12 g

Fat: 4 g

Ingredients:

2 Cups of Quinoa – Rinsed

4 Cups of Water

Dash of Salt

1 Cup of Pomegranate Seeds

½ tsp. of All Spice – Powdered

½ Cup of Mint – Chopped

Pine Nuts – Toasted

Dash of Lime Juice

1 Tbsp. of Olive Oil

Salt and Pepper – To Taste

Directions:

Put the quinoa, dash of salt, and water into the cooker. Toast the nuts while you wait.

Remove the rice and stir in the all spice and the lime juice. Allow it to cool.

Add in the other ingredients.

Jalapeno Bread

Calories: 75

Carbohydrates: 2 g

Protein: 2 g

Fat: 1 g

Ingredients:

2 ½ Cups of Flour

1 tsp. of Yeast

1 ½ Tbsp. of Sugar

1 ½ tsp. of Salt

1 ½ Tbsp. of Butter

2 Tbsp. of Milk

¾ Cup of Water

¾ Cup of Jalapeno – Chopped

½ Cup of Cheddar Cheese – Shredded

Directions:

Put the yeast in a bowl with the sugar and ¼ cup of warm water.

Let it sit for ten minutes. (It will look foamy.)

Put the flour sugar, and salt into the cooker and mix it.

Add in the milk and then the yeast mixture. Mix it well.

Put the butter in the middle of the dough.

Top it with the jalapeno.

No Meat Black Bean Chili

Calories: 417

Carbohydrates: 22 g

Protein: 27 g

Fat: 5 g

Ingredients:

1 Tbsp. of Olive Oil

2 Carrots – Diced

½ Onion – Diced

2 Cloves of Garlic – Crushed

2 Cans of Black Beans – Drained, Rinsed

1 Can of Black Beans – Not Drained

2 Tbsp. of Chili Powder

1 Tbsp. of Cumin

1 Can of Vegetarian Refried Black Beans

1 Large Can of Tomatoes

1 Cup of Vegetable Broth

Dash of Salt

Shredded Cheddar Cheese

Chopped Avocado

Directions:

Sauté the onions with the oil in a large pot on medium heat.

Add in the carrots and the garlic. Cook them until they are soft.

Add it all into the cooker with the broth, cumin, tomatoes, and the chili powder. Put your cooker on the quick setting for 20 minutes.

Add in the black beans and then cook on quick for another 20 minutes.

Add in the refried beans and then stir it.

Leave the cooker on warm.

Serve it with the cheese and avocado on top.

Pomegranate Pear Halves

Calories: 252

Carbohydrates: 43 g

Protein: 6 g

Fat: 6 g

Ingredients:

2 Pears – Firm, Halved

2 Cups of Pomegranate Juice

2 Cups of Apple Cider

1 – 3" Cinnamon Stick

Peel from 1 Clementine

2 Whole Cloves

2 Star Anise

3 Black Pods – Cardamon

1 – 1" Piece of Ginger – Peeled, Sliced

Orange Cashew Cream

Directions:

Put the pomegranate juice, cinnamon stick, apple cider, clementine peel, star anise, cloves, cardamom pods, and the ginger. Put the pear halves in there.

Close your cooker and cook it on white rice for 50 minutes.

Open and turn the pears. Let it sit for 1 hour.

Turn them over and allow them to set for another hour.

Refrigerate them for one night.

Serve with Orange Cashew Cream.

Shrimp with Lemon Risotto

Calories: 434

Carbohydrates: 47 g

Protein: 31 g

Fat: 11 g

Ingredients:

2 Tbsp. of Extra Virgin Olive Oil

5 tsp. of Butter – Divided

1 Cup of Onion – Chopped

1 Tbsp. of Lemon Zest – Finely Grated

1 Cup of Arborio Rice

¼ Cup of White Wine

3 Cups of Chicken Broth

12 Medium Shrimp – Peeled, Deveined

1 Cup of Blanched Corn Kernels

3 Tbsp. of Lemon Juice

½ Cup of Parmesan Cheese

Dash of Pepper

1 Tbsp. of Parsley – Chopped

4 Lemon Wedges

Dash of Salt

Directions:

Put the rice cooker on Quick Cook.

Add in the oil and 1 Tbsp. of butter. Sauté the onion for 3 minutes, and then stir in the lemon zest.

Stir in the rice and sauté it for 4 minutes.

Stir in the wine and cook it for 3-4 minutes.

Stir in the broth.

Cook it for 20 minutes.

Fold in the shrimp, lemon juice, and corn. Set the timer for 5 minutes.

Fold in the rest of the butter.

Season it with the salt and the pepper.

Fold in the Parmesan Cheese.

Balsamic Dijon Chicken and Farro with Mushrooms

Calories: 435

Carbohydrates: 25 g

Protein: 31 g

Fat: 6 g

Ingredients:

4 – 5 Ounce Chicken Breasts – Boneless, Skinless

1 tsp. of Olive Oil

2 Shallots – Minced

8 Ounce Cremini Mushrooms

1 Cup of Farro

1 ½ Cups of Vegetable Broth – Low Sodium

¼ Cup of Parsley – Minced

Marinade

1/3 Cup of Balsamic Vinegar

1 tsp. of Extra Virgin Olive Oil

1 Tbsp. of Dijon Mustard

Dash of Sea Salt

Dash of Pepper

Directions:

Prepare the marinade and put the chicken in a plastic bag with the marinade.

 Set the cooker to the regular setting.

Put 1 tsp. of oil in the cooker.

Add in the shallots. Cook them for 5 minutes.

Add in the mushrooms and cook them for 8 minutes.

Stir in the faro and cook it for 3 minutes.

Stir in the broth and put the chicken in the cooker without the left over marinade.

Cook it for 1 hour.

Recipe Junkies Alert!

Sign up for Recipe Junkies FREE Newsletter today and never pay more than a buck for a brand new recipe book! Receive alerts about new recipe books before they even come out! We have many other awesome offers for subscribers eyes only! You can follow us on Facebook and Twitter as well! Come be a part of the Recipe Junkies family where recipes are our business and business is good! You are more than just a number to us and we appreciate all of our newsletter subscribers.

<u>Recipe Junkies Alert Promo</u>
<u>Recipe Junkies Facebook</u>
<u>Recipe Junkies Twitter</u>

Wheat Berry Salad

Calories: 132

Carbohydrates: 34 g

Protein: 11 g

Fat: 2 g

Ingredients:

1 Cup of White Wheat Berries – Soft

2 Cups of Water

Dash of Salt

Directions:

Toast the berries in a pan for 4 minutes.

Drain the rice.

Cook in the cooker with 2 cups of rice and a dash of salt.

Frittata and Summer Vegetables

Calories: 177

Carbohydrates: 10 g

Protein: 8 g

Fat: 12 g

Ingredients:

1 Clove of Garlic – Peeled, Whole

1 Small Yellow or Red Onion - Diced

1 Small Potato – Peeled, Finely Chopped

1 Small Zucchini – Sliced

Dash of Salt

Dash of Pepper

1 Tbsp. of Olive Oil

6 Large Eggs – Beaten

2 Tbsp. of Cheese – Your preferred kind.

Directions:

Heat the oil in a pan.

Add in the garlic clove till its brown and then throw it away.

Add in the vegetables.

Season them with the salt and pepper. Then put them aside.

Put 1 Tbsp. of oil in the cooker.

Spread it all around the bottom and 2 inches up the side.

Add the eggs, cheese, salt, and the pepper.

Add in the vegetables.

Put the cooker on regular rice setting.

Vegetable Hot Cakes

Calories: 272

Carbohydrates: 23 g

Protein: 13 g

Fat: 4 g

Ingredients:

1 Egg

½ Cup of Milk

1/3 Cup of Carrots – Finely Chopped

1/3 Cup of Kobacha – Boiled, Cooled, Finely Chopped

1/3 Cup of Spinach – Boiled, Drained, Finely Chopped

1 Pack of Hot Cake Mix

Directions:

Mix everything together.

Set the cooker to regular.

Cook for 5-10 minutes.

Crazy Cheesy Polenta

Calories: 295

Carbohydrates: 26 g

Protein: 33 g

Fat: 7 g

Ingredients:

2 Tbsp. of Butter

½ Onion – Chopped

1 Clove of Garlic – Minced

1 Cup of Chicken Broth

1 Cup of Milk

½ Cup of Polenta

¼ tsp. of Salt

2 Ounces of Shredded Cheddar Cheese

2 Ounces of Shredded Parmesan Cheese

¼ tsp. of Pepper

Directions:

Put the butter, garlic, and the onion in the cooker.

Close the lid and cook it for 10-15 minutes.

Add in the chicken broth, polenta, milk, and salt.

Cover it and cook it for 20 minutes.

Add in the cheese, pepper, and Parmesan cheese.

Stir it until the cheese melts.

Easy Chicken Curry

Calories: 268

Carbohydrates: 27 g

Protein: 23 g

Fat: 6 g

Ingredients:

2 Tbsp. of Oil

1 Cup of Onion – Chopped

1 Tbsp. Garlic – Minced

2 Tbsp. of Curry Powder

2 Cups of Water

1 – 8 Ounce Can of Tomato Sauce

1 – 8 Ounce Package of Zatarain's Jambalaya Mix

1 Pound of Chicken Breasts – Boneless, Skinless, Cubed

½ Cup of Golden Raisin

¾ Cup of Plain Yogurt

1/3 Cup of Cashews – Chopped

Directions:

Push the cook button and add the oil.

Put the garlic and the onions and cook them for 5 minutes.

Add the curry powder and cook it for 2 minutes.

Add in the water, Jambalaya Mix, tomato sauce, chicken, and raisin mix.

Cook it.

Kimichi

Calories: 154

Carbohydrates: 15 g

Protein: 9 g

Fat: 2 g

Ingredients:

1 Small Napa Cabbage – Cubed

1 Daikon Radish – Julienned

6 Thai Chiles – Minced

2 Cloves of Garlic – Minced

½ Cup of Green Onions – ½ inch Pieces

2 Tbsp. of Ginger – Grated

½ Cup of Sea Salt

2 Tbsp. of Unseasoned Rice Vinegar

1 tsp. of Sugar

Directions:

Fill the pot with 2 cups of water and add in the salt.

Add the cabbage and stir it.

Close the lid and allow it to sit for 24 hours. Stir it occasionally.

Drain the cabbage and mix in the ingredients.

Can it and seal it.

Allow it to sit for 3 days.

Seafood Steamer Rice

Calories: 312

Carbohydrates: 31 g

Protein: 25 g

Fat: 8 g

Ingredients:

15 Pieces of Prawns – Shells Removed, Deveined

3 Pieces of Squid – Washed, Cubed

2 Cups of Rice – Wash, Drained

3 Cups of Water

2 Star Anise

3 Cm Cinnamon Stick

3 Cloves

3 Tbsp. of Golden Raisin

2 cm Turmeric – Crushed

1 Tbsp. of Garlic – Sliced

2 Kaffic Leaves

3 Tbsp. of Oil

Cashews – Garnish

Seasoning:

1 tsp. of Curry Powder

1 tsp. of Salt

½ tsp. of Sugar

Directions:

Heat the oil, sauté the turmeric, garlic, cloves, cinnamon stick, and the star anise.

Put the rice in the cooker.

Put the mix in the pot.

Add in the squid, prawns, golden raisin, seasonings, and the kaffic leaves.

Add in enough water to cover the rice.

Cook it, and then garnish it with the cashews.

Zesty Corn Dip

Calories: 197

Carbohydrates: 27 g

Protein: 27 g

Fat: 7 g

Ingredients:

4 Ears of Corn

6 Slices of Bacon – Cooked, Crumbled

2 Cups of Sour Cream

8 Ounces of Cotija Cheese

4 ½ Ounce Can of Chopped Chilies

4 ½ Ounce Can of Jalapenos – Chopped

½ Cup of Scallions – Thinly Sliced

Dash of Salt

Dash of Pepper

Directions:

Add in 2 cups of water into the cooker.

Steam it for 15 minutes.

Add in the corn and steam it.

Mix in all f the ingredients and allow it to stand in the fridge over night.

Whole Chicken

Calories: 224

Carbohydrates: 21 g

Protein: 26 g

Fat: 4 g

Ingredients:

1 – 2-3 Pound Chicken

2 Small Onions – Peeled

1 Lemon

2 Rosemary Sprigs

2 Tbsp. of Butter

Dash of Salt

Dash of Pepper

Directions:

Cut the onions in half and put them with the flat side down in the cooker.

Cut the lemon in half and put it inside the chicken with the rosemary.

Coat your chicken with the butter and season it with salt and the pepper.

Put the chicken in the cooker on top of the onions.

Set it to White Rice. Cycle it again if you need to.

Clam Chowder

Calories: 423

Carbohydrates: 32 g

Protein: 24 g

Fat: 12 g

Ingredients:

2 Tbsp. of Butter

1 Cup of Onion – Chopped

1 Cup of Celery – With Leaves, Chopped

2 Cloves of Garlic – Chopped

2 Cups of Potatoes – Cubed

1 Tbsp. of Flour

2 Cups of Vegetable Stock

1 Cup of Heavy Cream

1 – 16 Ounce Can of Clams – Chopped

1 Bay Leaf

1 Thyme Sprig

Directions:

Set the cooker to sauté and brown the onion, garlic, and celery for 5 minutes.

Add in the flour and mix it well.

Pour the vegetable stock in with the bay leaf.

Add in the thyme and the potatoes.

Allow it to simmer for 20 minutes.

Add in the cream and the clams with the clam juice.

Cook it for another 10 minutes.

Traditional Hummus

Calories: 223

Carbohydrates: 24 g

Protein: 30 g

Fat: 7 g

Ingredients:

2 Cups of Garbanzo Beans – Dry

1 Tbsp. of Tahini

3 Tbsp. of Olive Oil

1 tsp. of Cumin

1 tsp. of Coriander

2 Cloves of Garlic

¼ Cup of Lemon Juice

Dash of Salt

Dash of Pepper

Directions:

Soak the beans over night in 6 cups of water.

Rinse the beans and put them in the rice cooker.

Cover the beans with water 1 inch above.

Cook them on the White Rice setting.

Use a food processor to blend them. Add in the lemon juice, salt, pepper, and oil.

Sweet Corn on the Cob

Calories: 174

Carbohydrates: 22 g

Protein: 13 g

Fat: 4.5 g

Ingredients:

1 ½ Cup of Water

Fresh Corn – Trimmed, Halved

Directions:

Put the corn in the steam tray.

Add in 1 ½ Cup of water.

Steam them for 10 minutes.

Steamed Sweet Potatoes

Calories: 231

Carbohydrates: 21 g

Protein: 11 g

Fat: 5 g

Ingredients:

1 Pound of Sweet Potatoes

2 Cups of Water

Directions:

Peel and cut the potatoes into cubes.

Put 2 cups of water in the pot.

Steam them for 17 minutes.

Southern Corn Pudding

Calories: 323

Carbohydrates: 21 g

Protein: 11 g

Fat: 8 g

Ingredients:

2 Cups of Water

1 – 11 Ounce of Creamed style Corn

2 Cups of Milk – Low Fat

2 Large Eggs – Well Beaten

3 Tbsp. of Sugar

½ tsp. of Salt

2 Tbsp. of Flour

1 Tbsp. of Butter

Directions:

Put 2 cups of water in the inner pot of your cooker.

Bring the water to a boil; this will take 8 minutes.

In a medium-mixing bowl, add in the milk, corn, sugar, eggs, flour, and the salt.

Pour the batter into the cooker. Put the butter on top.

Cover it with aluminum foil and cook it for 45 minutes.

Steamed Mussels with Black Bean Sauce

Calories: 347

Carbohydrates: 24 g

Protein: 31 g

Fat: 11 g

Ingredients:

1 Pound of Mussels – Cleaned

2 Cups of Water

2 Tbsp. of Water

1 tsp. of Brown Sugar

3 Cloves of Garlic – Minced

1 Tbsp. of Ginger – Minced

2 Green Onions – Chopped Fine

2 Tbsp. of Red Bell Pepper

2 Tbsp. of Green Bell Pepper

½ tsp. of Fish Sauce

¼ Cup of Cilantro – Chopped

Directions:

Put the 2 cups of water in the inner pot.

When it begins to steam, put the mussels in the cooker and cook them for 6-8 minutes.

If the mussels don't open, cook longer.

Remove them and put them on a platter.

Make the black bean sauce by sautéing 2 Tbsp. of water and the rest of the ingredients for 1-2 minutes.

Add it to the mussels and stir them gently.

Steamed Green Beans

Calories: 44

Carbohydrates: 10 g

Protein: 3 g

Fat: 0 g

Ingredients:

1 Pounds of Green Beans

2 Cups of Water

Directions:

Add 2 cups of water into the inner pot.

Add in the green beans and steam them for 10-12 minutes.

Butternut Squash Steamed

Calories: 82

Carbohydrates: 22 g

Protein: 2 g

Fat: 0 g

Ingredients:

1 Pound of Butternut Squash – Peeled, Cubed

2 Cups of Water

Directions:

Add 2 cups of water into the inner pot.

Add in the squash to the cooker.

Cook it for 10-12 minutes.

Spicy Cheese Dip

Calories: 80

Carbohydrates: 5 g

Protein: 1 g

Fat: 6 g

Ingredients:

1 Small Onion – Chopped

1 Small Jalapeno Pepper – Chopped

1 Tomato – Seeded, Chopped

1 tsp. of Olive Oil

½ Cup of Mexican Beer

12 Ounces of Pepper Jack Cheese – Grated

4 Ounce of Sharp White Cheddar – Grated

Directions:

Set the cooker to sauté and add in the oil.

Fry the jalapeno, onion, and tomato until its soft.

Add in ½ of the beer and cook it until it evaporates.

Add in the cheese and the rest of the beer and melt it together.

Lemongrass with Shrimp Soup

Calories: 65

Carbohydrates: 7 g

Protein: 9 g

Fat: 5 g

Ingredients:

1 Pound of Jumbo Shrimp – Peeled, Deveined

2 Carrots – Sliced

2 Celery Stalks – Sliced

½ Onion – Sliced

2 Cloves of Garlic – Sliced Thin

2 Large Sliced of Ginger

2 Tbsp. of Red Pepper Flakes

1 Lemongrass Stalk

4 Cups of Vegetable Broth

2 Tbsp. of Coconut Oil

Directions:

Remove the tough and leaves of the lemongrass stalk.

Cut it in 2-3 Inch Pieces

Set the cooker to sauté and then add in the oil.

Add the vegetables, garlic, and ginger to the cooker. Sauté it for 10 minutes

Add in the broth and the red pepper flakes. Allow it to cook for another 10 minutes.

Add in the shrimp and cook it for another 2 minutes.

Spanish Rice

Calories: 61

Carbohydrates: 7 g

Protein: 4 g

Fat: 2 g

Ingredients:

3 Cups of White Rice – Uncooked

1 ½ Pound of Vegetable Crumble

1 Medium Onion – Chopped

1 Small Can of Diced Green Chilies

1 Regular Can of Tomatoes – Diced

1 Small Can of Tomato Sauce

1 tsp. of Chili Powder

Dash of Salt

Dash of Pepper

Directions:

Prepare the rice like you should with the cooker.

Cook the vegetable crumbles with the onion.

Add in the rest of the ingredients to the cookers.

Cook it for another 5 minutes.

Spaghetti Squash and Kale with Pancetta

Calories: 265

Carbohydrates: 17 g

Protein: 9 g

Fat: 7 g

Ingredients:

½ Spaghetti Squash – Seeded

2 Cloves of Garlic – Chopped

½ Cup of Pancetta – Chopped

1 Onion – Chopped Finely

2 Cups of Kale – Chopped, Ribs Removed

¼ Cup of Parmesan Cheese – Grated

Directions:

Put ½ of the squash in the inner pot with 2 cups of water.

Steam it for 20 minutes.

Remove the squash and put it aside.

Cook the onion, pancetta, and garlic for 10 minutes.

Add in the kale and cook it for 3 more minutes.

Scrap the strings from the squash and toss it with the kale, garlic, onion, and pancetta mix.

Smoked Salmon Frittata

Calories: 232

Carbohydrates: 9 g

Protein: 8 g

Fat: 3 g

Ingredients:

6 Large Eggs

4 Ounce of Smoked Salmon

1 tsp. of Butter

2 Tbsp. of Cilantro

Dash of Pepper

Directions:

Whisk the eggs and pepper in a bowl.

Pour the eggs into the inner pot and put the salmon and herbs on top.

Close the lid and cook it for 5 minutes.

Shrimp and Girts

Calories: 296

Carbohydrates: 30 g

Protein: 27 g

Fat: 6 g

Ingredients:

1 Pound of Shrimp – Peeled, Deveined

½ Onion – Chopped

1 Clove of Garlic – Minced

2 Tbsp. of Butter

¼ Cup of Beer

2 Pieces of Bacon – Chopped

1 Cup of Yellow Grits – Instant

1 Cup of parmesan Cheese

¼ Cup of Butter

Dash of Salt

Dash of Pepper

Directions:

Put 2 cups of water in the cook and set it to steam.

When it starts to boil, stir in the grits and cook it for 5 minutes.

Add in the butter and the cheese. Set it aside.

Brown the bacon and crumble it.

Add the onion and the garlic and cook it until its soft.

Add in the shrimp and the beer. Cook it until its done.

Add in the salt and the pepper.

Serve the shrimp on top of the grits.

Savory Lentils

Calories: 276

Carbohydrates: 23 g

Protein: 6 g

Fat: 14 g

Ingredients:

2 Tbsp. of Extra Virgin Olive Oil

½ tsp. of Curry Powder

1 tsp. of Cumin

1 Cup of Brown Lentils – Washed

2 2/3 Cups of Water

1 – 14 Ounce Can of Tomatoes – Diced with Juice

2 Tbsp. of Onion – Minced

1 Tbsp. of Vegetable Flakes

2 Tbsp. of Parsley

Dash of Salt

Dash of Pepper

Directions:

Add in all of the ingredients to the inner pot and mix it.

Set the cooker to White Rice setting and cook it.

Half way through, mix it.

Allow it to stand for 10 minutes.

Rice San Antonio Style

Calories: 189

Carbohydrates: 30 g

Protein: 10 g

Fat: 3 g

Ingredients:

1 Cup of White Rice

1 – 12 Ounce Jar of Salsa

1 Tbsp. of Vegetable Oil

1 Cup of Corn Kernels

½ tsp. of Cumin

½ tsp. of Salt

Dash of Pepper

1 ¼ Cups of Water

Fresh Cilantro

Directions:

Add in all of the ingredients. (Not the cilantro.)

Stir it together and cook it on the White Rice setting.

Allow it to stand 8-10 minutes. Garnish it with cilantro.

Potato and Salmon Gratin

Calories: 348

Carbohydrates: 25 g

Protein: 26 g

Fat: 15 g

Ingredients:

4 Large Potatoes – Thinly Sliced

16 Ounce Can of Wild Salmon

1 Cup of Milk

1 Egg

2 Tbsp. of Butter

Dash of Salt

Dash of Pepper

Directions:

Add butter to your inner pot.

Put the potato slices in the cooker.

Spoon ¼ of the salmon on top of the potatoes.

Sprinkle it with salt and pepper.

Repeat it in layers.

Mix in the milk and egg in a bowl.

Pour it on the potatoes.

Cook it for 60 minutes.

Orange Marmalade

Calories: 49

Carbohydrates: 13 g

Protein: 0 g

Fat: 0 g

Ingredients:

2 Cups of Oranges – Unpeeled

2 Cups of Sugar

Directions:

Cut the oranges into chunks. Remove the white, thick center.

Put the oranges and the sugar into the cooker.

Sauté them for 15 minutes.

Put the marmalade in a sterile jar.

Pinto Beans

Calories: 245

Carbohydrates: 44 g

Protein: 15 g

Fat: 1 g

Ingredients:

2 Cups of Pinto Beans

6 Cups of Water

2 Tbsp. of Salt

Directions:

Rinse and soak the beans in water overnight.

Drain and rinse the beans.

Put the water, the beans, and the salt in the pot.

Cook it on the white rice setting.

Rice Pineapple Pudding

Calories: 309

Carbohydrates: 34 g

Protein: 5 g

Fat: 10 g

Ingredients:

1 ¾ Cups of Vanilla Rice Non-Dairy Beverage

1 ¼ Cups of Water

Dash of Salt

¾ Cup of Jasmine Rice

1/3 Cups of Sugar

4 Ounces of Egg Substitute

1 tsp. of Vanilla Extract

1 – 8 Ounce Can of Crushed Pineapple with the juice

Directions:

Pour 1 cup of the rice dream and the water into the inner pot.

Cook it on white rice setting. Allow it to boil.

Stir in the rice and the salt. Allow it to stand for at least 30 minutes.

In a small mixing bowl, whisk the ¾ cup of rice dream, egg, sugar, and vanilla.

Stir in the pineapple with the juice.

Stir the egg mixture with the rum.

Allow it to simmer until it is thick.

Peppermint Truffles

Calories: 210

Carbohydrates: 19 g

Protein: 2 g

Fat: 14 g

Ingredients:

8 Ounces of Dark Chocolate – Chopped

¼ Cup of Heavy Cream

2 Drops of Peppermint Extract

1 Cup of Candy Canes – Crushed

Directions:

Add 1 cup of water to the inner part of the pot.

Put a clear bowl on the pot.

Set it to steam and add in the chocolate with the cream. Mix it as it heats.

When the chocolate is melted, add in the peppermint extract.

Put the bowl in the refrigerator for at least 1 hour.

Let it sit out for 2 hours.

Scoop out small ball sized portions and roll them around.

Put the crushed candy canes inside the bowl and drop 2 truffles in at one time. Roll them around to coat them.

Barley Pearled Stuffing

Calories: 149

Carbohydrates: 32 g

Protein: 5 g

Fat: 1 g

Ingredients:

1 Cup of Pearled Barley – Cooked

2 Stalks of Celery – Chopped

1 Onion – Chopped

4 Cloves of Garlic

4 Bacon Slices – Cooked, Crumbled

2 Sprigs of Thyme

½ Cup of Cranberries – Dried

2 Cups of Old Bread – Cubed (Or Croutons)

2 Eggs

1 Cup of Chicken Stock

2 Tbsp. of Butter

Directions:

Add in 1 cup of barley with 2 cups of water into the inner part of the cooker.

Select Brown Rice setting and allow it to cook.

Add the bacon, celery, onion, and garlic to the cooker.

Cook it for another 5 minutes.

Add in the bread.

Press the Cake button and close the lid.

Pasta Carbonara

Calories: 307

Carbohydrates: 45 g

Protein: 19 g

Fat: 7 g

Ingredients:

6 Slices of Thick Bacon – Sliced Thin

½ Cup of Onion – Diced

1 Clove of Garlic

1 Egg

2 Cups of Heavy Cream

1 Cup of Parmesan Cheese – Shredded

4 Cups of Pasta

2 tsp. of Salt

1 tsp. of Pepper

Directions:

Set the cooker to Brown Rice.

Brown the garlic, onions, and the bacon. Put it aside.

Add in 8 cups of water to the inner part of the pot. Set it to steam for 7 minutes

Add in the pasta and cook it.

Drain the noodles and put the pasta back in.

In a medium-mixing bowl, add in the eggs, the cheese, and the cream. Whisk them well.

Put the mix into the pasta and mix it.

Add in the pepper and the bacon mix.

Cook it for another 5 minutes.

Orange Rice Pilaf

Calories: 179

Carbohydrates: 28 g

Protein: 4 g

Fat: 5 g

Ingredients:

1 Cup of White Rice

2 Tbsp. of Butter – Unsalted

¼ Cup of Onion – Chopped Fine

Juice from 2 Oranges

1 ¾ Cups of Chicken Broth

½ tsp. of Salt

¼ Cup of Toasted Almonds

Directions:

Add in all of the ingredients to the inner part of the cooker. (Except for the almonds.)

Cook it for 20 minutes.

Allow it to stand for 10 minutes.

Top it with almonds.

Midnight Omelet

Calories: 475

Carbohydrates: 4 g

Protein: 28 g

Fat: 38 g

Ingredients:

1 Tbsp. of Green Onion – Sliced Thin

2 Tbsp. of Cilantro – Diced

½ Cup of Vegetables

1 tsp. of Butter

2 Tbsp. of White Mushrooms – Diced

3 Large Eggs – Beaten

1 Tbsp. of Half and Half

½ Cup of Cheddar Cheese – Shredded

Dash of Salt

Dash of Pepper

Directions:

Close the lid and steam it to preheat it for 10 minutes.

Put the butter and the mushroom in the inner part of the pot.

Add in the green onions, vegetables, and the tomatoes.

Sauté it for 2 minutes.

In a small mixing bowl, whisk the eggs, salt, cream, and pepper.

Pour it on the vegetables and stir it gently.

Close the lid and cook the eggs for 12-14 minutes.

Sprinkle the cheese on top. Fold the eggs over.

Lemon Dill Rice

Calories: 307

Carbohydrates: 45 g

Protein: 19 g

Fat: 7 g

Ingredients:

1 Cup of White Rice

1 ¾ Cups of Water

½ tsp. of Salt

Zest of 1 Lemon

1 Tbsp. of Lemon Juice

½ tsp. of Dried Dill

1 tsp. of Parsley

2 Tbsp. of Butter

Dash of Salt

Dash of Pepper

Directions:

Add all of the ingredients to the inner part of the cooker.

Set it to the White Rice setting.

Let it stand for 10 minutes before you serve it.

Classic Quiche

Calories: 362

Carbohydrates: 30 g

Protein: 19 g

Fat: 8 g

Ingredients:

4 Eggs

¼ Cup of Heavy Cream

½ Cup of Cheese – Shredded

½ Cup of Pancetta – Chopped

½ Cup of Onion – Chopped

1 Cup of Collard Greens – Chopped

Dash of Pepper

1 Cup of Bread

Directions:

Brown the onions, greens, and the pancetta in the cooker.

Remove them and set it aside.

Add in the bread. Mix in the eggs, cheese, and the cream to the pancetta mixture.

Pour it on the bread.

Add a dash of pepper.

Cook it on White Rice setting.

Brussels Sprouts with Walnut Oil

Calories: 163

Carbohydrates: 19 g

Protein: 11 g

Fat: 6 g

Ingredients:

1 Pound of Brussels Sprouts – Halved

½ Cup of Almonds – Chopped

2 Shallots – Thinly Sliced

1 Clove of Garlic

½ Cup of Cranberries – Chopped

1 Tbsp. of Agave Syrup

1 Tbsp. of Walnut Oil

1 Tbsp. of Olive Oil

Dash of Salt

Dash of Pepper

Directions:

Set the cooker to Sauté and sauté the Brussels sprouts for 5 minutes.

Add in the shallots and the garlic. Cook them for another 3-4 minutes.

Add in the cranberries, ½ cup of water, and the agave. Let it cook for another 5 minutes.

Toss in the almonds, salt, pepper, and the walnut oil.

Vegetarian Easy Penne Peasy

Calories: 207

Carbohydrates: 32 g

Protein: 7 g

Fat: 3 g

Ingredients:

3 Cups of Whole Grain Penne Pasta – Mini

1 Can of White Beans

1 Small Can of Tomato Sauce

1 Can of Tomatoes with Chiles – Diced

1 Can of Tomatoes – Diced

½ Cup of Sweet Onion – Diced

2 Cups of Broccoli – Diced

1 Tbsp. of Garlic – Minced

½ Cup of Radish – Minced

2 Cups of Vegetable Broth

1 Cup of Water

Directions:

Stir all the ingredients together and cook it on the White Rice setting.

Stir it 2 times during cooking.

Vegetarian Noodle Soup

Calories: 321

Carbohydrates: 41 g

Protein: 12 g

Fat: 6 g

Ingredients:

1 Tbsp. of Olive Oil

1 Clove of Garlic – Minced

1 Onion – Chopped

3 Carrots – Sliced

14 Ounces of Peas – Drained

15 Ounces of Tomatoes – Drained, Pureed

5 Ounces of Vegetable Juice

¼ Cup of Water

3 Tbsp. of Red Wine

2 Tbsp. of Vegetarian Worcestershire Sauce

2 Cups of Farfalle Noodles

1/8 tsp. of Country Herb Blend

Dash of Salt

Dash of Pepper

Directions:

Preheat the cooker on Steam for 10 minutes.

Add in the oil, garlic, and onion. Stir it until it is tender.

Add in the rest of the ingredients.

Cook it for 25 minutes.

Rice Thai Style

Calories: 237

Carbohydrates: 31 g

Protein: 10 g

Fat: 4 g

Ingredients:

1 Cup of Long Grain Jasmine Rice

2 Cups of Canned Coconut Milk

¼ tsp. of Cardamom

½ tsp. of Coriander

¼ tsp. of Salt

Directions:

Add in all of the ingredients to the inner part of the pot.

Cook it on the White Rice setting.

Allow it to stand for 10 minutes.

Swiss Rice Pie

Calories: 332

Carbohydrates: 35 g

Protein: 13 g

Fat: 9 g

Ingredients:

½ Cup of Long Grain Rice

½ Cup of Sugar

½ tsp. of Salt

1 Tbsp. of Butter – Unsalted

3 Cups of Milk

2 tsp. of Lemon Zest

½ Cup of Almonds – Finely Chopped

1 Tbsp. of Flour

3 Large Eggs – Beaten

Sugar

1 Pie Crust

Flour for Dusting

Directions:

Prepare the rice per the instructions.

Add the milk and butter with ½ cup of sugar and the salt to a pan and bring it to a boil on medium heat.

Turn the heat to low and simmer it for 25 minutes.

Allow it to cool and then puree it in the food processor.

Pour it into a mixing bowl with the lemon zest, almonds, and 1 Tbsp. of flour.

Stir in the eggs.

Put it in the cooker and cook it on the White Rice setting.

Spanish Rice

Calories: 307

Carbohydrates: 45 g

Protein: 19 g

Fat: 7 g

Ingredients:

2 Cups of Long Grain Rice

1 ½ Cup of Chicken Broth

1 Small Onion – Diced

2 Cloves of Garlic – Minced

7 Ounces of Tomato Sauce

10 Ounces of Tomatoes with Chili Peppers – Diced

½ tsp. of Cumin

½ tsp. of Pepper

1 Habanero Pepper

Directions:

Mix all of the ingredients together and cook them on the White Rice setting.

Allow it to stand for 10 minutes.

Now who on earth would possibly give a rotten review to a book with this fuzzy little guy inside of it?

Check out other best sellers on Amazon from the Recipe Junkie family...

Recipe Junkies Alert!

Sign up for Recipe Junkies FREE Newsletter today and never pay more than a buck for a brand new recipe book! Receive alerts about new recipe books before they even come out! We have many other awesome offers for subscribers eyes only! You can follow us on Facebook and Twitter as well! Come be a part of the Recipe Junkies family where recipes are our business and business is good! You are more than just a number to us and we appreciate all of our newsletter subscribers.

Recipe Junkies Alert Promo

Recipe Junkies Facebook

Recipe Junkies Twitter

These recipes are not intended to be any type of Medical advice. ALL diabetics must consult their Doctors first and should always receive their meal plans from a qualified practitioner. . These recipes are not intended to heal, or cure anyone from any kind of illness, or disease.

Printed in Great Britain
by Amazon